Remember to Pray

Remember to Pray

Remember to Pray

Remember to Pray

Remember to Pray

Wider, Longer, Higher, Deeper

Forty Days of Prayer, Scripture, and Growth-filled Questions

Paul M. Burns

Remember to Pray

Remember to Pray

Remember to Pray

Remember to Pray

Remember to Pray

Remember to Pray

Preface

What is this book?

Wider, Longer, Higher, Deeper contains forty days of themes, scripture readings, thoughtful quotes, and growth-filled questions. It is inspired by the prayer found in Ephesians 3:17–18:

> *I pray that you, being rooted and established in love, may have power, together with all the Lord's holy people, to grasp how wide and long and high and deep is the love of Christ* (NIV).

Why questions instead of reflections?

The greatest growth I have experienced in my own faith and witnessed in others has come from wrestling with profound questions. Any wisdom I may share in this book is limited to my own experience. Great insight into God and self is found in plumbing the deep waters of one's own soul, bathed in the light of scripture and sought diligently through contemplation and prayer.

How might I proceed?

Consider using the daily devotion to begin or end your day, either in solitude or with a partner. When you pray, ask God to illumine your mind and heart to receive a word about God, yourself, and your relationships with others. End with a prayer for wisdom and courage to take a step forward in faith.

Remember to Pray

Carefully read and meditate on the scripture before moving to the quote or questions. Think about how you reflect most deeply. Is it in conversation? In writing? Through song? While cooking? Carry the questions with you throughout the day. The best questions often take time to answer.

May God open you ever wider in mercy, ever longer into life, ever higher into the heavens, and ever deeper into love.

— Paul Burns

Day 1

The Creation of Relationship
Genesis 2:18–25

Helped are those who create anything at all, for they shall relive the thrill of their own conception and realize a partnership in the Creation of the universe that keeps them responsible and cheerful.
— Alice Walker

1) All throughout the creation story God "saw that it was good." What is the first thing God saw as being not good and why?

2) Why do you think the man eventually chose the woman to be his helping partner instead of one of the animals?

3) What helping partners do you have in fulfilling God's mission on earth? How do they help you?

Day 2

Laughing Partners

Genesis 18:1–5, 21:1–7

The secret of seeing is to sail on solar wind. Hone and spread your spirit, 'til you yourself are a sail, whetted, translucent, broadside to the merest puff.
— Annie Dillard

1) Whom were you with the last time you had a good laugh? Why did you laugh?

2) Have you ever had a period in your life when you didn't laugh much? Why?

3) What promises has God made to you? Are they fulfilled or unfilled?

Day 3

Making Amends Out of a Mess

Genesis 16:1–11, 21:8–21

Compassion is sometimes the fatal capacity for feeling what it is like to live inside somebody else's skin. It is the knowledge that there can never really be any peace and joy for me until there is peace and joy finally for you too. — Frederick Buechner

1) To whom do you relate most in this story: Abraham, Sarah, Hagar, Ishmael, or God? Why?

2) How did God intervene in this mess? How has God intervened in your messes?

3) Have you ever had to let go of a relationship? Have you entrusted this person to God?

Day 4

Facing Forgiveness

Genesis 32:1–12, 33:1–11

Blessed is the servant who loves his brother as much when he is sick and useless as when he is well and being of service to him. And blessed is he who loves his brother as well when he is afar off as when he is by his side, and who would say nothing behind his back he might not, in love, say before his face.
— St. Francis of Assisi

1) It had been over twenty years since Jacob had seen his brother Esau. How do you think time had changed them?

2) How have you been affected by holding a grudge? How did it affect your other relationships?

3) If you have reconciled with a person, how did it change you? If you have not, what is stopping you from doing so?

Day 5

Motherly, Brotherly Love

Genesis 50:15–21

The heart of a mother is a deep abyss at the bottom of which you will always find forgiveness. — Honoré de Balzac

1) What would you have done in Joseph's situation?

2) How do you love others like a mother? Like a brother or a sister?

3) Would you rather be God's servant or friend? Why? What difference might it make?

Day 6

The Spirit of Adoption

Romans 8:12–17

I believe in Christianity as I believe that the sun has risen; not only because I can see it, but because by it I see everything else. — C. S. Lewis

1) In what ways are you indebted to anything or anyone other than God?

2) What does it mean to you to be adopted as a child of God?

3) What does being an heir of God the Father along with Christ have to do with suffering?

Day 7

A Trinity Relationship

Ruth 1:1–18

Friendship is born at that moment when one person says to another, "What! You too? I thought I was the only one." — C. S. Lewis

1) Have you had a Naomi in your life who has taken you under her or his wing?

2) Have you been a Naomi to someone else?

3) How is Ruth like Jesus?

Day 8

Lifelong Parenting

1 Samuel 3:10–21

The right way to approach God is to stretch out our hands and ask of One who we know has the heart of a Father. — Dietrich Bonhoeffer

1) How would you describe the relationship between Eli and Samuel?

2) Have people who were not your parents helped raise you? Who and how?

3) How can you help parent today's children?

Day 9

God between Us

1 Samuel 18:1–5, 20:41–42

"We'll be friends forever, won't we Pooh?" asked Piglet. "Even longer," Pooh answered. — A. A. Milne

1) How does Jonathan's love for David help equip him for being king someday?

2) Do you have a Jonathan in your life who loves you deeply and whole-heartedly?

3) In what ways do you hold back your love for others? Why?

Day 10

The Pleasure and the Pain

Song of Solomon 2:8–17, 8:6–7

When I was a boy of 14, my father was so ignorant I could hardly stand to have the old man around. But when I got to be 21, I was astonished at how much the old man had learned in seven years. — Mark Twain

1) What have been the most pleasurable and painful moments in your life?

2) When have you felt most vulnerable to or intimate with another person?

3) What do you need in order to consider your sexuality a gift from God to be celebrated instead of a source of shame and pain?

Day 11

A Relationship of Discovery

John 1:35–51

Life without a purpose is a languid, drifting thing; every day we ought to review our purpose, saying to ourselves, "This day let me make a sound beginning, for what we have hitherto done is naught!" — Thomas á Kempis

1) What are your gifts?

2) How did you discover them?

3) How can you use your gifts for God?

Day 12

A Sign for the Times
John 2:1–12

If I were to wish for anything, I should not wish for wealth and power, but for the passionate sense of the potential, for the eye which, ever young and ardent, sees the possible. Pleasure disappoints, possibility never. And what wine is so sparkling, what so fragrant, what so intoxicating, as possibility! — Søren Kierkegaard

1) Do you find yourself focusing more on the past, the present, or the future? Why?

2) What keeps you from fully enjoying what God has given you?

3) What does it mean to you to trust God with the timing of your life?

Day 13

A Match Made in Heaven

John 3:1–15

With Christ, we have access in a one-to-one relationship, for, as in the Old Testament, it was more one of worship and awe, a vertical relationship. The New Testament, on the other hand, we look across at a Jesus who looks familiar, horizontal. The combination is what makes the Cross. — Bono

1) Which of your relationships do you feel were meant to be?

2) How did they come about?

3) If Jesus were sitting right next to you, what do you think he would say to you, and what would you say to him?

Day 14

Renewable Relationship

John 4:1–15

A promise is a cloud; fulfillment is rain. — Arabian proverb

1) When have you felt as if you were out of gas?

2) What resources do you use to fill up your tank? Is your relationship with Christ one of them?

3) If Christ is your fuel source, how do you share that relationship with others?

Day 15

Open Doors

John 4:16–30

The God who existed before any religion counts on you to make the oneness of the human family known and celebrated. — Desmond Tutu

1) What about yourself are you afraid to reveal? How does it make you feel to know Christ already knows all about it and still loves you?

2) How are you an open door to Christ? What about to other people?

3) In what ways have others opened their doors to you? And how do you share Christ with others?

Day 16

A Friend in Need...

John 5:1–15

A friend in need is a friend indeed. — Traditional proverb

1) Have you ever tried to help someone who has given up trying to get better? How did it go?

2) Have you ever been helped in a time of need by a stranger? How did it feel?

3) How can you be a friend to a stranger in need even if you cannot help?

Day 17

It's All about Trust

John 4:46–54

Christian faith is a grand cathedral, with divinely pictured windows. Standing without, you can see no glory, nor can imagine any, but standing within, every ray of light reveals a harmony of unspeakable splendors. — Nathaniel Hawthorne

1) When did you first believe God is real? What or who triggered your belief?

2) What events have helped your faith grow?

3) When have you needed your faith the most?

Day 18

Holding on to Stones
John 8:1–11

If you judge people, you have no time to love them.
— Mother Teresa

1) Whom do you have the greatest tendency to judge and want to condemn? Why?

2) What do you feel others judge or condemn you for?

3) What might it look like to replace judgment and condemnation with compassion and mercy?

Day 19

The Value of Blindness

John 9:24–41

Humility is not thinking of yourself, it's thinking of yourself less. — C. S. Lewis

1) In what ways have you been blind?

2) In what ways can your eyes deceive you?

3) In what ways might you see Jesus more clearly?

Day 20

All In

John 11:1–16

We're never so vulnerable than when we trust someone—but paradoxically, if we cannot trust, neither can we find love or joy. — Walter Anderson

1) What does it mean to completely trust a person?

2) What does it mean to completely trust God?

3) What might your life look like if you completely trusted God?

Day 21

Living in a World without End
John 11:17–27

Be not afraid of life. Believe that life is worth living and your belief will help create the fact. — William James

1) What do you do to console those who have experienced great loss?

2) Do you believe in resurrection? What difference does it make to believe in it or not?

3) If you knew you would never die, how would you live your life differently?

Day 22

An Unbound Life

John 11:28–44

Our greatest glory is not in never failing, but in rising up every time we fail. — Ralph Waldo Emerson

1) How have you grown from failure and heartache?

2) In what ways would you like to grow spiritually?

3) Finish this statement: I could be more useful to God if . . .

Day 23

Living Sacrifice

John 12:1–8

The person who risks nothing does nothing, has nothing, is nothing, and becomes nothing. He may avoid suffering and sorrow, but he simply cannot learn and feel and change and grow and love and live. — Leo Buscaglia

1) In what ways have you experienced unconditional love?

2) What are the costs and risks of loving unconditionally?

3) What might be the costs and risks of loving God unconditionally? How different might your life look if you loved God in this way?

Day 24

Footwork

John 13:1–20

If there is no humility, love remains blocked, it cannot go forward. — Pope Francis

1) What is the hardest thing about loving others?

2) Who are people who have metaphorically washed your feet?

3) Whose feet is God calling you to wash?

Day 25

A Way Paved with Trust

John 14:1–14

The best way to find out if you can trust somebody is to trust them. — Ernest Hemmingway

1) Whom do you trust the most and why?

2) What does it mean to you to trust in Jesus Christ?

3) How different might your life look if you fully trusted in Jesus Christ?

Day 26

One Spirit, Many Names

John 14:15–26

Isn't it amazing that we are all made in God's image, and yet there is so much diversity among his people? — Desmond Tutu

1) If the Holy Spirit is God present in the world today, how have you experienced or witnessed him?

2) Who in your life has been your advocate? Helper? Teacher? Partner? Counselor? Comforter? Intercessor? Strengthener? Standby? Friend?

3) How can you fill these roles for these others?

Day 27

Cultivating Love

John 15:1–17

Keep love in your heart. A life without it is like a sunless garden when the flowers are dead. The consciousness of loving and being loved brings a warmth and richness to life that nothing else can bring. — Oscar Wilde

1) How has the love of others affected your life?

2) What events in your life have made you more loving toward others?

3) Name the three people you find hardest to love. How might you learn to love them?

Day 28

To Whom Do You Belong?

John 15:18–27, 16:33

There are always two choices. Two paths to take. One is easy. And its only reward is that it's easy. — Harry S. Truman

1) In what ways is your life different because you follow Christ?

2) In what ways does the "world" compete for your time, talent, and money?

3) What might it look like for you to fully belong to God?

Day 29

Label-Free Zone

John 17:1–9, 17:20–23

A miracle is heaven spilling out into our mundane reality. — Paul Burns

1) What labels do you wear? What labels do you place on others?

2) What labels can all humanity share? What labels can all followers of Christ share?

3) What do you hope guests experience at your home or church?

Day 30

Here Is Your Family

John 19:25b–30

You don't choose your family. They are God's gift to you, as you are to them. — Desmond Tutu

1) What does it mean to *be* family?

2) Who has been family to you?

3) How can you expand your family?

Day 31

God Is for Us

Isaiah 40:1–11

True peace is not a balance of opposing forces. It is not a lovely "façade" which conceals conflicts and divisions. Peace calls for a daily commitment, starting from God's gift, from the grace which he has given us in Jesus Christ. — Pope Francis

1) Has there been a time in your life when you felt God was against you?

2) What does it mean to know that God is for you?

3) In what ways can you be for others?

Day 32

God Is with Us

Matthew 1:18–25

God loves each of us as if there were only one of us.
— St. Augustine

1) Can you think of a time in your life when you absolutely knew God was with you?

2) What does it mean to you to be with people?

3) In what ways can you embody God when you are with people?

Day 33

Becoming One

Ephesians 1:1–10

Do you want to do something beautiful for God? There is a person who needs you. This is your chance. — Mother Teresa

1) If you could wish for one thing and knew it would absolutely come true, what would your wish be?

2) How would this one thing change the world?

3) What one thing could you do this year that might change the world?

Day 34

Lifetime Beneficiaries

Ephesians 1:10–14

This is all the inheritance I give my dear family. The religion of Christ will give them one which will make them rich indeed. — Patrick Henry

1) In what ways has God blessed you?

2) In what ways do you bless others?

3) How can you make room for more people in your life?

Day 35

High-Powered

Ephesians 1:15–23

Never forget that the most powerful force on earth is love. — Nelson Rockefeller

1) How does knowing Jesus impact your life?

2) What does it mean to you to call Jesus *Lord*?

3) In what ways can you know Jesus better?

Day 36

Alive and Working

Ephesians 2:1–10

If we are saved by grace, then why are we working so hard? — Josephine Crenshaw

1) Can you remember a time when you did pretty much exactly what you wanted, when you wanted?

2) At what point did God's agenda become more important to you than your agenda or someone else's agenda for you?

3) What do you feel God is calling you to do at this point in your life?

Remember to Pray

Day 37

Reconciling Differences

Ephesians 2:11–16

The number one problem in the world is alienation, rich versus poor, black versus white, labor versus management, conservative versus liberal, but Christ came to bring about reconciliation and peace. —
Billy Graham

1) What subjects do you find put you at odds with other people?

2) Have you lost a relationship over one of those subjects?

3) What might it look like to make Christ the center of all your relationships?

Remember to Pray

Day 38

A Work in Process

Ephesians 2:17–22

Life is a process of becoming a combination of states we have to go through. Where people fail is that they wish to elect a state and remain in it. This is a kind of death. — Anaïs Nin

1) How have you changed in the last five, ten, twenty, thirty, fifty years?

2) How have you become more like Christ over time?

3) In what ways would you like to become more like Christ in the next five, ten, twenty, thirty, fifty years?

Day 39

Captivated by Grace

Ephesians 3:1–13

The Church is the Church only when it exists for others . . . not dominating, but helping and serving. It must tell men of every calling what it means to live for Christ, to exist for others. — Dietrich Bonhoeffer

1) If you had to describe yourself in one sentence, what would you say?

2) If you could only say one sentence to people for the rest of your life, what would it be?

3) What might your God-given mission be?

Day 40

Wider, Longer, Higher, Deeper

Ephesians 3:14–21

It's like trying to describe what you feel when you're standing on the rim of the Grand Canyon or remembering your first love or the birth of your child. You have to be there to really know what it's like. — Jack Schmitt

1) In what ways is God making you more accepting of others? Pushing you to reach out further to others? Giving you a bigger perspective? Pulling you deeper into relationship?

2) In what ways are you resisting God in his expansion of you?

3) What needs to happen for you to fully receive God into your life?

Remember to Pray

Remember to Pray

Made in the USA
Coppell, TX
13 December 2023

26039134R00030